TIGERS

TIGERS

by

Guy Mountfort

CRESCENT BOOKS
NEW YORK

0-517-133628
LCCCN 73-92288

Printed in Great Britain
by Colorgraphic Limited, Leicester

Contents

Preface

Although very few people have seen tigers in the wild, they are paradoxically among the most widely known animals in the world – in zoos or circuses, in story-books, as emblems of majesty, as advertising symbols, or as hunting trophies. Much of our knowledge and many misconceptions about the tiger were obtained over the barrel of a gun. But George Schaller, a brilliant young American scientist, has studied their behaviour in depth and I am deeply indebted to him for some of the information and two of the pictures in this book.

Although I have studied tigers in the wild in several countries, I lay no claim to any new discovery about their way of life. That they impress me constantly by their sheer magnificence I freely admit. I am also convinced of their importance, as predators, to the balance of animal communities in Asia; without them the deer and wild pig populations would be neither kept in check nor healthy. Experiencing so much enjoyment in studying tigers, I find it difficult to understand how anyone can take pleasure in killing them, despite the evidence to the contrary in the many books written by hunters.

Today the tiger is facing extinction. But although uncontrolled shooting, trapping and poisoning were important factors in this, they were not the primary cause. Like all animals, including man, the tiger's survival depends on the maintenance of a delicately balanced ecosystem and a stable environment, both of which are now being destroyed. The once vast forests of Asia, teeming with animal life, which provided its food and shelter, are rapidly disappearing to make way for the ever-increasing human population. Loss of habitat is therefore the chief reason for its decline. Today we face the realisation that there are just too many people on our tiny planet – our over-exploited and polluted biosphere.

Conservation, in a nutshell, means the wise use of natural resources. It does not mean putting the needs of wildlife before human needs. On the contrary it aims to preserve the beauties and the diversities of nature as essentials to human existence. Forty years from now the human population will have doubled. Our need for escape from the concrete jungle in which much of mankind will by then be living will be acute. It was to ensure that wildlife and wilderness would survive this pressure that the World Wildlife Fund was created. It provides what *Time*

Magazine aptly described as 'a kind of United Nations for conservation', by raising money internationally and spending it on a scientifically assessed priority basis, wherever it is most urgently needed. Already it has completed 840 vitally important conservation projects in seventy-seven countries. Among its current projects is a carefully planned programme to save the tiger from extinction. In the latter part of this book I have given the background to this dramatic last-minute effort, in which many nations are helping the governments of India, Nepal, Bhutan and Bangladesh to create a number of new, scientifically managed wildlife reserves. Tigers do not 'belong' to any one nation. They are part of our inheritance of natural treasures, which we despoil or exterminate at our peril. It is as important that we should regard their survival as the responsibility of the whole civilised community, as that nations should co-operate, as they do, to protect the man-made treasures of the world. If the necessary finance can be raised (it represents no more than the cost of half a mile of motorway) the tiger *could* be saved for posterity. If not, the tiger is doomed.

I hope that those who read this book will regard the effort – the international crusade to save the tiger – as worthy of support.

GUY MOUNTFORT

1 The tiger-king of beasts

December dawn in the Kanha National Park. It is one of the few small areas in India's vastness where tigers can still feel relatively safe. Opalescent mist hangs like a fluffy blanket over the descending slopes of the meadow below the bungalow. Two shaggy vultures, their plumage still wet with dew, sit hunched and motionless, black against the brightening sky. Their perch on a dead tree rises disembodied above the whiteness. A string of big-antlered barasingha deer leaves the distant stream reluctantly, heading for the safety of the trees. On the rising slope beyond, the tall sal forest is already noisy with bird voices.

We clamber into the Land-Rover, muffled against the cold and disbelieving that the temperature will rise to 85°F before midday. Over the rickety bridge and turning off the rutted track, we enter a long grassy glade into the forest. Our stately elephants stand patiently waiting at the far end. At a word from the *mahouts* they kneel, ponderously, like skyscrapers collapsing in slow motion. We sit back-to-back in the *howdahs*, our legs dangling above the gently heaving flanks. Binoculars and cameras are readied and we begin to plod noiselessly into the trees. The teatray-size feet below us are placed with careful precision, the sensitive 'fingers' on the massive trunks daintily testing the ground ahead. A tiger has made a kill during the night and we are hoping to catch sight of it.

The tangle of low branches brushes our faces as we descend the hillside towards the stream. The warden knows where the kill was made and the elephants spread out to approach from different angles. Commands are now whispered, but most of the steering is done by the bare feet of the *mahouts* planted behind the elephants' ears.

We halt, and our elephant begins a quiet, subterranean rumbling. She smells tiger and, though willing to obey her master, cannot quite suppress an inbred dislike for it. A nudge from the bare heels and she moves a few more steps forward. The stream and the kill are in view.

Although none of us except our elephant has spotted it, a tiger rises from a patch of yellow withered grass, seizes the 400-pound carcass of a young buffalo by the neck and walks away with it, without apparent effort, into a clump of bamboo. The warden whistles briefly and gesticulates to the other *mahouts*, who slowly walk their elephants to circle behind the bamboo. We wait, our elephant motionless but still rumbling anxiously, for we are much closer.

Presently, as the circling elephants approach, the tiger emerges. He stands looking at us suspiciously and then begins to walk towards us. He is unhurried. We watch, entranced, as the huge form, rippling with muscle, weaves in and out of the undergrowth, finally passing through the trees on our right, within thirty paces. There is no sound but the clicking of our camera shutters. The tiger does not look up as he passes, but heads for some long grass. There to our delight, he lies down in a patch of sunlight, on his side with his feet towards us. He blinks his greenish eyes lazily, though the tip of his tail is twitching a little nervously. From the slope above we have a grandstand view. He is lithe, magnificent, and the quintessence of feline grace. We note the characteristic white spot in the centre of the black ear, the tremendous breadth of the powerful fore limbs, the handsome ruffles behind the cheeks, and the black-and-white patterning above the eyes, by which each tiger can be distinguished from its neighbours. But it is the superb gleaming satin of the sun-dappled orange-and-black fur which most impresses us by comparison with the appearance of zoo tigers.

The tiger yawns cavernously, stretching his chin vertically and pulling back his lips to expose his formidable canines. We continue to watch for ten minutes and then the warden, anxious for closer portraits, urges our elephant forward. Like an unleashed spring, the tiger is in motion and vanishes.

A fully grown male tiger is a huge animal. Unlike lions, which are social, moving about in prides of anything up to thirty, including cubs, tigers are solitary, hunting usually at night. For this reason they are infinitely more difficult to locate or to observe. Lions are typical occupants of the open savannah of central Africa. Tigers are much more adaptable and accept a much wider choice of habitat. In China they occupy coniferous forests and high-grass thickets; in their western range they can be found in tamarisk forests, reed beds and marshes; in the hills of Manchuria in birch, scrub-oak and walnut thickets; in high rain-forest in Indo-China, Burma and Malaya; grass thickets in Cambodia and Thailand; humid mangrove swamps in Sumatra and the Indo-Bangladesh Sunderbans; and from dry thorn to deciduous tropical evergreen forests in other parts of India. In fact almost anywhere, fulfilling their three cardinal requirements: ample cover and a sufficiency of fresh water and prey species. They have been found in deep snow at −30°F in Manchuria and their tracks have been seen in the Himalayan foothills between Nepal and Sikkim at 13,000 feet above sea level. Throughout these differing regions the tiger was once the dominant predator, fearing only its arch-enemy, man. And today man has succeeded in harassing this most magnificent of creatures to the verge of extinction.

Few, if any, wild animals have had so much written about them, though most of the books were written from experience gained over the barrel of a gun. The famous Jim Corbett was the greatest of these writers. From time immemorial hunters have regarded tigers as the epitome of savagery and ferocity and hence as their most prized trophies. To kill a tiger with a bow and arrow was the ultimate demonstration of courage by Far Eastern tribal hunters long before the shotgun was invented, and there is evidence from artefacts of 3000 BC that it was even then probably regarded as the king of beasts.

Throughout the zoos of the world the tiger is a popular attraction, providing a pleasurable thrill as it paces helplessly back and forth in its iron and concrete dungeon, deprived of everything it most needs but food. Yet, unlike the lion, which is seen basking in the sunlight of the African reserves by millions of tourists, the tiger has been seen in the wild by relatively few people from the western world. It has scarcely been studied objectively and in depth in its wild state, though informative books about it were written by Burton (1933) and Perry (1964). The exception was the brilliant work of the young American scientist George Schaller (1967), who followed the daily lives of tigers in India, unarmed and usually on foot, for months on end. His book is a model of factual

11

analysis of behaviour and entirely free both of guesswork and romanticism.

Schaller showed that in areas where tigers are not constantly persecuted, they are no more dangerous or liable to attack a human who is not threatening them than any other wild animal. Forsyth (1889) and Fletcher (1911) had taken the same view, but few believed them at the time. With good reason, tigers have learned to fear man. They are more likely to move away than to be aggressive, though they often show curiosity. Even when occasionally a tiger felt irked by Schaller's presence near its kill and made a bounding run towards him, it changed its mind and retreated. On one occasion he found himself within ten feet of a tiger, which, though startled, merely walked away. On another occasion he came suddenly face to face around a rock at four feet. The tiger was as astonished as he was and it gave a growling roar. This time it was Schaller who retreated – at first rapidly but quietly, and then, as the tiger followed, he climbed a tree. The tiger was joined by three grown cubs and for half an hour the animals sat and watched him. Eventually he shouted at them and they all scampered away. They had been curious rather than threatening.

I myself have been very close to a tiger when walking with a friend in the remote Terai of western Nepal. My companion, once a well-known big-game hunter and now an ardent conservationist, was completely unperturbed. We were in an area of ten-foot grass among tangled trees when we heard the unmistakable coughing 'woof' of a tiger close behind us. Had it had aggressive intentions, escape would have been impossible. We stood still and after a few more uneasy moaning notes the tiger withdrew and lay down for a siesta. And we continued our walk. On the previous night at our camp near the river we had heard a tiger roar. We slept near the camp fire under an open tarpaulin shelter to avoid the heavy night dew. In the morning we found the tracks of a big tigress within twenty-four feet of my camp cot. After inspecting the camp it had moved on. Our baggage included no fire-arms.

The tiger probably originated in the region of Manchuria. Its range stretched some 6,000 miles across Asia, from eastern Turkey to the China Sea, gradually extending to hotter climates through the Indian subcontinent and the Indonesian islands as far south as Bali, though neither Borneo nor Ceylon were colonised. It was well known in India even before the ancient Hindu Veda scriptures were written.

Today the species *Panthera tigris* is generally divided into eight races, or subspecies. These range in size from the big Siberian tiger *P. t. altaica*, which is said to have reached the record length of 13 feet, to the smaller southern races which barely exceed 9 feet. The females are smaller. Adult weights vary greatly, from an exceptional 705 pounds down to as little as 350 pounds; the average is probably 420 to 450 pounds. The skin of a lion is dull and of varying shades of tawny or brownish-buff, the male having a heavy, dark mane, the long hair often extending below as far as the belly. By contrast, a healthy tiger, particularly in the southern races, has a coat with a satin-like sheen, though this is often absent in conditions of captivity. The bold black striping against the rich golden-orange background, with white on the face, belly, and inner surfaces of the legs, is a combination which looks very conspicuous in a cage. But it provides perfect cryptic camouflage in the animal's normal habitat. A tiger standing still in long, parched grass almost dissolves from view, while even in the green jungle the alternation of black and orange merges astonishingly well into the pattern of broken sunlight and dense shadow.

I was once watching a tiger when my attention was diverted momentarily by the scolding of some langur monkeys overhead. When I reverted to the tiger, which had not moved, it took me several seconds to relocate it, so perfectly did it merge with its surroundings. This colouration is, of course, of paramount importance in enabling the tiger to stalk its prey. Stories of tigers 'charging' their prey in the open are largely fictional. The normal practice is to approach by stealth, creeping slowly forward while taking advantage of every shred of cover until within twenty or thirty feet. If the prey is grazing in an open tract of grass and the tiger cannot find sufficient cover for a close approach, it will lie hidden until the animal draws near enough. Then, with a short rush, the victim is toppled over or pulled down by the tremendously powerful fore paws and killed either by a bite through the nape of the neck, or, in the case of a large animal such as a buffalo, by being seized by the throat until it strangles, its head meanwhile being held on the ground.

Tigers maintain large hunting ranges, which they patrol at night, using the same route regularly and thus often falling victims of pit-traps, or of hunters armed with spotlights and rifles. Schaller found that they covered between ten and twenty miles in a night. The frequency with which they kill prey varies according to availability and the size of the prey, two large animals or three smaller ones per week probably being a fair average. One might say that the tiger preys on almost anything it considers worth killing, though preferring various deer and wild oxen and the wild boar. It will eat fish, birds, reptiles, and any domestic animal. Even the elephant and rhinoceros may be attacked if other prey is scarce, and tigers sometimes kill and eat each other. They occasionally kill leopards and not infrequently bears. It should be remembered in the tiger's favour that as the dominant Asian predator it plays an essential role, both in helping to control numbers in the wild ungulate populations, and in maintaining their virility by weeding out the weakly and more easily caught individuals.

The tiger's appetite is voracious. Schaller calculated by carefully weighing carcasses that it often eats the equivalent of one-fifth of its own body weight, say sixty pounds of meat, during one night's feasting. An adult domestic cow can be completely disposed of in three nights, only the head and lower part of the legs remaining. Vegetable matter in the stomach is left, but the intestines and smaller bones are eaten. Tigers have few natural enemies, but a full-grown wild boar has been known to disembowel them and a pack of wild dogs (the Indian dholes) can sometimes succeed in killing them, though only after numerous casualties. There are also records of tigers dying a lingering death after incautiously attacking the big Indian porcupine, which, instead of fleeing, backs into them and drives its long quills into the throat and lungs. Tigers like water and swim readily. Though not normally tree-climbers they are known to be able to climb them in extreme emergency, such as escaping a flood; undoubtedly many did so during the cyclonic flooding of the Sunderbans in 1969, as so very few were found drowned. At least one hunter

14

has been seized by the leg when eighteen feet up in a tree. I spent two nights tiger-watching from a *machan* hide twelve feet up in a tree in the Sunderbans – and was afterwards told that it was much too low for safety from the man-eaters of that region.

2 The problem of the man-eater

Night-time in the Sunderbans. The setting moon hangs low over the Pussur River, which slides, glass-smooth on its way to the Bay of Bengal, between the overhanging sundri trees and graceful golpatta palms. The tide is ebbing, exposing along the muddy shores a million sharp bayonets – the spike-like pneumatophores, or air-roots, by which the mangroves obtain the life-giving oxygen which they cannot extract from the muddy, saline water. Among the regiments of spikes, fiddler crabs are already excavating their holes and waving their monstrously enlarged single claws. The little amphibian mud-skipper fish, too, are beginning to exchange the comparative safety of the river for the more dangerous element of the open air as dawn approaches, 'rowing' themselves forward on the wet mud with their limb-like pectoral fins. But the junglecocks, the heralds of day, have not yet begun to crow and the stillness of night is broken only by the high, nervous bark of a chital stag.

Tied up at the bank is a slender canoe, its sleeping occupant shrouded against the heavy dew. He has paddled all day from his little stilted bamboo hut at Chandpai village to reach this spot. Tomorrow he will join his companions on the ancient fishing boat with the carved prow lying in the shallows near Tiger Point. He has seven children and is desperately poor. Like his companions he is deeply in debt to the *mahajans*, the rich money-lenders to whom the catch is always mortgaged in advance at usurious rates. When his daughters marry he will have to borrow again for their dowries. When he dies, his debts will be passed on to his sons and they, too, will probably be in debt all their lives. It is the custom, and beyond complaining.

Again the chital barks and stamps. It scents danger. Minutes pass and in the failing moonlight near where the canoe is tied, the massive head of a tiger materialises under the arching branches. The cold, greenish eyes are on the canoe and the ears are pricked forward. Noiselessly, placing its great paws with precision between the sharp pneumatophores, the tiger advances to the water's edge, calculating the distance. Twenty feet of water separated the canoe from the bank when it was tied up at dusk. Barely nine feet of water now remain. The tiger crouches, its feet deep in the mud, and with an easy leap is in the canoe, which nearly capsizes under the 400-pound onslaught. There is a brief, muffled cry and the tiger wades back out of the river, carrying the limp body of the fisherman by the neck, as nonchalantly as if it had been a goat. Fifty yards inside the shelter of the trees it drops the body and begins eating it, starting as usual at the buttocks.

A few weeks later, a patrolling forest guard notices the empty canoe and lands to investigate. The track where the body was dragged is still visible, and in the little trampled clearing is the fisherman's tattered and blood-stained *lungi*. Scavengers have removed what the tiger did not eat. When, a few days later, the guard reaches a telephone, he reports his discovery to the police and the Department of Forests at Khulna. Careful entries are made on official forms about the unknown fisherman who was a victim of the man-eaters of the Sunderbans. An officially recognised victim, that is, for empty canoes are often found in the vast wilderness of mangroves. Some of their occupants are doubtless killed by tigers, but unless there is evidence these do not appear in the statistics. Men can die without trace by many different means in these parts, from family feuds or drowning, to snake-bites or piracy.

Although my admiration for tigers is boundless, it would be stupid to pretend that they are harmless animals. They are carnivores which kill with terrifying efficiency and their stalking skill is unsurpassed. The toll they levy on domestic animals when their natural prey is not available can be very heavy. Schaller estimated that, although game was fairly plentiful in the Kanha National Park, ten resident tigers killed 250 head of domestic cattle in or near the park, in twelve months. And, of course, some tigers become man-eaters.

Normally this occurs only rarely, as a result of injury or old age preventing them from successfully hunting wild animals, or when deprived of their usual prey. Unfortunately, so much dramatic literature has been devoted to man-eaters that many people assume the habit to be widespread. This has led to such comments as that written by the hunter Inglis in 1892: 'The tiger is the embodiment of devilish cruelty, of hate and savagery incarnate.' Such a view is anthropomorphic and misleading.

In 1902, when tigers were still very numerous throughout India, government statistics showed that 1,046 people out of a population of some 250 millions had been killed by tigers; but this does not mean that there were more than a few hundred man-eaters in the country. When the habit develops, it usually persists and the behaviour can be taught to the cubs of the family. There are records of scores of people having been killed by the same animal. But today a man-eater does not survive for long and it is usually quickly shot before it can claim another victim. Bounties are still paid for killing them and many an innocent tiger is shot along with the real culprit. To put man-eating in perspective, one must remember that deaths by snake-bite in India outnumber those caused by tigers by more than twenty to one.

Today only in the Sunderbans is man-eating a persistent problem and there it is undeniably serious. In the last ten years 275 men are known to have died by this cause. The habit is known to date back at least to 1665, and long before the Sunderbans was denuded of large prey species such as the gaur bison, the rhino and the barasingha. Wild boar and chital are still fairly plentiful, though far below their previous numbers. Shortage of food is therefore not the cause of the problem, though today perhaps contributing to its continuance.

Obviously the widespread habit of man-eating by the Sunderbans tigers must have a particular reason. After receiving the report of my expedition there, the trustees of the World Wildlife Fund consulted Professor Paul Leyhausen, chairman of the Cat Specialist Group of the International Union for Conservation of Nature and Natural Resources. By his initiative and with money provided by the WWF, it was decided to send a scientist to study the ecological factors which might have a bearing on the subject. The man chosen, Dr Hubert Hendrichs, was able after a first reconnaissance of only three months to draw tentative conclusions. Although these need careful confirmation by more detailed study, on which he is now engaged, they seem unlikely to be disproved. First it was clear that there was a positive correlation between man-eating and ferocity with the level of salinity in the water and the height of the water level. Second was a negative correlation with the available variety of vegetation and mammal fauna. Third, it seemed probable that the high level of salt in the aquatic habitat of the Sunderbans, ingested for countless generations by the tigers, may have caused physiological changes, notably damage to the liver and kidneys. The local fresh-water sources are very restricted. Dr Hendrichs confirmed my belief that persistent man-eating was confined to only part of the tiger population and that although occasional humans occurred in all areas, there were considerable tracts of forest where no human casualties had been recorded.

It now seems that a problem which has puzzled experts for many years may soon be solved. We may also have the key to a gradual reduction of human losses by the introduction of appropriate management techniques. The aim of these will be to conserve human life, forest utilisation *and* the tiger. Dr Hendrichs has already suggested what steps might be taken and these should not be difficult to achieve. However, confirmation of his theories must first be obtained.

3 The present status of the tiger

Reliable information about the present status of the tiger is very difficult to obtain. One might be forgiven for imagining that such a large animal would be a relatively easy subject for head-counting. Animals such as the African rhinos, which inhabit open country, or elephant seals which breed colonially, present little difficulty. One can count migrating caribou or wildebeest with reasonable accuracy by aerial photography. But the tiger is self-effacing and lives in terrain which provides ample cover and difficult access.

I gained an impression of the difficulty of making even approximate estimates of the tiger population during the World Wildlife Fund expedition to the Sunderbans in 1967. A local hunter told me there were 500 tigers in the 3,500 square miles of mangrove jungle. The Department of Forests, whose guards patrolled the area regularly, said there were 300. We attempted a census based on transects by motor launch back and forth through the area, during which all sightings, kills, tracks, faeces and vocalisations were carefully noted. As a statistical exercise it was a failure. Our launches could not negotiate many of the shallow creeks. Although the daily tidal exposure of the mud shores enabled us to distinguish between fresh and old pug-marks, the creeks were too numerous and time too short for us to distinguish for long the tracks of individual tigers. Nevertheless and even allowing for unexplored areas, we gained a clear impression that the total probably did not exceed one hundred. Local *shikaris* were vociferous in scorning our estimate when it was published, but I have since heard no evidence to disprove it.

How many tigers in all, then, are thought to remain in Asia?

Of the eight races, one, the Bali tiger, *P. t. balica*, is already extinct. It was still common in 1914, but by 1920 was reduced to rarity. No steps were taken to protect it and by 1937 the last one was reported to have been shot.

Rumour persists that one or two may still survive but during my visit in 1973 I found nothing to support this.

The Siberian tiger, *P. t. altaica*, is a tremendously powerful animal, heavier in the head and fore-quarters than any other race and with longer fur. It is thought to have occupied the whole area of the Amur River basin and its upper water-courses, including the tributary river systems of the Bureya, Zeya, Ussuri and Sungari-Nonni. Today in the Soviet Far East it survives in only a few isolated regions of the Amur valley south of the Bureya range and in the middle and upper reaches of the Khor and Bilkin rivers among the Sikhote-Alin mountains. A few may still exist in north-eastern China, in the mountains of Kirin and Heilungkiang Provinces. Between 1957 and 1966 there were only five known occurrences of this race in northern Korea, since when nothing more has been heard from that country. The most recent estimate of the total population surviving (1972) was 130 in the Soviet Far East and *perhaps* a small number scattered through north-east China and Korea. It is unlikely, however, that many tigers survived the Korean War.

Efforts have been made to save the remaining Siberian tigers in the USSR. They were given legal protection in 1948 and the wild ungulates which provide their prey have also been protected in order to reduce predation on domestic livestock. Even stricter protection was given in the big Sikhote-Alin and Sudzukhe Reserves. But by 1964 only the pug-marks of two nomadic tigers passing through could be found and it was concluded that the resident populations in the reserves had disappeared, though there has since then been some recovery. In spite of every protective measure, a few Siberian tigers are still being shot every year in the Soviet Far East, and as late as 1964, fifteen wild-caught young were exported to zoos. Even if present plans to enlarge the Sikhote-Alin Reserve are implemented and efforts are made to re-stock it, the total remaining number of tigers of this race may now be too small to maintain a viable breeding population.

The neighbouring Chinese race, *P. t. amoyensis*, is a smaller animal. Its coat is shorter and more richly coloured, with broader striping. The fur is nevertheless longer and softer than that of the typical Indian race. Because western explorers and hunters rarely travelled

21

in China (and not at all in recent times) we know very little about the Chinese tiger. It is thought that it used to be seen frequently in Kansu and Szechwan Provinces and may still be in southern Szechwan. The range is believed to extend eastward from the 38th to the 40th parallel, and southward through central and eastern China in the Province of Fukien and the Yangtse River valley. It is replaced by the Indo-Chinese race, *P. t. corbetti*, in the south of Yunnan, Kwangsi, and Kwantung Provinces. But much of this is speculative. All we can ascertain from Chinese sources today is that the race has become 'very rare'. This is scarcely surprising as it benefits by no kind of protection whatever. Indeed, according to the IUCN *Red Book of Endangered Species*, 'official Chinese policy encourages its destruction, as it is regarded as a menace to human life and a hindrance to agricultural and pastoral progress'. Moreover, within its range, every part of the tiger's carcass is 'highly esteemed by the Chinese for its alleged medicinal properties, for which reason it has long been assiduously hunted'.

There seems not the least doubt that the Chinese tiger will follow the Bali tiger into extinction in the very near future. As there are only fifteen Chinese tigers in captivity, scattered among various Chinese and Russian zoos, (and these may have been cross-bred with other races) the possibility of maintaining the race artificially is also just about zero.

Fortunately, the Indo-Chinese race, *P. t. corbetti*, may still present a relatively more cheerful picture. But only relatively, because it is everywhere known to be declining steeply. It is very unlikely that anything approaching the 1954 estimate of 3,000 is still accurate. Its range embraces a huge area, from southern China through Indo-China, Vietnam, Laos, Cambodia, eastern Burma, Thailand, and the Malay Peninsula to Singapore. Nearly 2,000 miles from north to south. Large parts of some of these countries have been totally devastated by modern warfare in recent years, not only by artillery and massive bombing with high explosives, but also by napalm and saturation with persistent arsenical defoliants. Incalculable losses have been inflicted on every form of living thing. Enormous tracts of virgin forest have been transformed into lifeless desert, so heavily poisoned that even humans with all their modern medical resources dare not reinhabit it for years to come. Tigers there undoubtedly were, in some numbers, in these areas; but few could have survived the holocaust of the fighting zones. We can only guess at the number remaining elsewhere. Wherever armies have camped or had lines of communication, every animal large enough to attract a shot from a trigger-happy or bored soldier has also suffered. War is hell for wildlife as well as humans.

The limitless forests of Burma and Thailand still contain tigers of the Indo-Chinese race; but forest exploitation, road-building, hunting and the skin trade are taking a heavy toll. If this race is to survive, it must be provided with large and completely protected reserves. At present existing reserves where tigers occur, such as Pidaung in Burma, Khao Salob, and Khao Yai in Thailand, and Taman Negara in Malaysia, are by no means adequately protected. This race of tiger may well outlive the others, but judged by today's situation it is difficult to believe it can escape extinction beyond the end of the present century unless its protection is greatly improved.

In the big island of Sumatra a different race occurs. The Sumatran tiger, *P. t. sumatrae*, is smaller and more fully striped than the Indo-Chinese or Indian races and with less white marking. Its stripes often degenerate into spots and its skull has a distinctively flattened profile. In 1936 it was still numerous even near thickly populated areas and, though obviously decreasing, was not considered to be in need of protection. By 1965 its status had seriously deteriorated. Today it survives only in the northern part of the island and the mountainous region of the south-west. No estimate of actual numbers is available, but it is certainly now in the very low hundreds. The destruction of its natural prey and the constant erosion of its habitat by the growing human population cause the tigers to prey increasingly on domestic livestock. Consequently they are vigorously hunted, not only with guns, but by means of baited cage-traps and pitfalls armed with bamboo spears. There are not yet reports of the poison bait which is causing such havoc in India, but doubtless this will follow. The Gunung Leuser is the only effective reserve for the tiger in Sumatra, though elsewhere it is supposed to be protected. It will be surprising if this race can survive the next thirty years.

In Java the situation is even more critical. The Javan

tiger, *P. t. sondaica*, is literally on its last legs. Like the Sumatran race it is a comparatively small animal, but with a generally darker ground colour. Its stripes tend to be narrower and closer together, or to be replaced by spotting; the insides and rear surfaces of the legs lack the dark marking of the Sumatran race. Its skull differs from those of all other races by the marked constriction of the occiput.

In 1851 tigers were plentiful in most parts of Java. The native human population apparently still regards them as the reincarnation of the souls of their departed kinsmen. One would therefore expect the tiger to be held in reverence and to be unmolested, if not vigorously protected. On the contrary, it is everywhere enthusiastically hunted. By the 1930s everyone could see that its numbers were dramatically declining. In 1921 the Netherlands Indies Government had created the Udjung Kulon Reserve to protect the disappearing Javan rhinos, the bantengs, and the tigers in that area; but no steps were taken to save the tigers elsewhere in the island. By 1940 they had become rare and the government introduced a system of permits for shooting them, though still allowing natives to kill them by any other means such as traps or poison. In district after district they were exterminated. By 1955 only twenty to twenty-five remained, a dozen of which were in the Udjung Kulon Reserve. By 1964 only twelve were left in the whole island. Latest reports put the total at between five and ten, all in the Betiri Forest Reserve. Though now officially protected, there can be little hope for the Javan tiger. Nor can the race survive for long in captivity, as only four of those held by various zoos are females. Nevertheless, it is encouraging that the Indonesian government is now making a last minute effort to save the remaining Javan and Sumatran tigers.

The prospect for the Caspian tiger, *P. t. virgata*, is equally depressing. Animals of this race are of medium size, with rather brownish, closely-striped fur, which is dense in texture and longish in winter. Until after the Russian Revolution, when land clearance and resettlement began on an increasing scale, the Caspian tiger had a huge range, from Mount Ararat and the Caspian eastward through northern Iran and Afghanistan to Sinkiang, and north to the Aral Sea, Lake Balkhash, the

Altai, and the Irtish Basin. To land clearance under the various Russian five-year plans was added a vigorous campaign to exterminate all wild animals likely to interfere with agricultural or pastoral developments. The number of hunters sky-rocketed. Special military task forces were given orders to concentrate on killing tigers; this was executed with such thoroughness that within a few years none remained throughout the greater part of their Russian range. At the same period the once magnificent Caspian forests and the vast reed thickets of the littoral, where many tigers lived, were almost wiped out to make way for rice, tea and cotton crops. By 1950 there were no Caspian tigers anywhere in the USSR, though a few vagrants continued to cross from Iran or Afghanistan until 1964. Strict protection for the tiger was introduced, but it was then too late.

In Iran the Caspian tiger is also now protected, but again too late. It is believed that about fifteen may remain in the Elburz mountains and just south of Gorgan; but the population is obviously now too small to offer any prospect of long survival. The continued shooting of wild boar, the principal prey species in Iran, is hastening the final conclusion.

Until recently, all hope of saving the Caspian tiger was concentrated on Afghanistan, where it was believed that perhaps a hundred or so still remained in the remote northern tugai forests of the upper Amu Dar'ya and Pyandzh basin. However, recent news suggests that there are now probably very few, if any, tigers left in Afghanistan. Apparently the last definite evidence of their presence was in 1965, when fresh pug-marks were identified on the banks of the Oxus at Dharkat, by a German scientific mission. So there seems little doubt that the Caspian tiger will soon be extinct everywhere.

Finally we come to the best known or Indian race, the so-called 'Royal' Bengal tiger. Because this form was the first to be described, it is called the nominate race, *Panthera tigris tigris*. It has been the favourite trophy of kings, princes, maharajahs, and sportsmen for many centuries. And what a history of man's stupidity and lust for killing can be found in the countless books about it! For a single sportsman to kill 300 or 400 tigers in a lifetime was not unusual. There was competition between the Indian princes to out-do each other in organising bigger and better tiger *shikars* and the bags were enormous. In 1965 at least one maharajah could claim personally to have shot 1,150 tigers during his lifetime. During the period of the British raj, tiger hunting was, as a matter of course, the pastime of nearly all army officers and government officials. Everyone behaved as though the supply was inexhaustible.

The Indian tiger is distinguished by its relatively short and glossy coat, with eighteen to twenty black stripes from shoulder to tail-root. The stripes are often double. There is frequently a short ruffle behind the cheeks. With its long limbs, rich colouration and strikingly lithe body it is usually regarded as the most beautiful of the cats of the world, though in my opinion the snow leopard must run it very close for this honour. The short, satin-like fur of the Indian tiger, so unlike that of the original shaggy northern race, is an evolutionary development reflecting the great heat to which tigers have adapted themselves in many parts of India. Even so, the Indian race is obliged to seek shade at the height of the day and obviously does not enjoy extreme temperatures.

The former distribution of the race included the Indus Valley of West Pakistan, which in the old days contained extensive tracts of bamboo, thorn forest and undergrowth, in regions which have since been converted into desert. The last tiger in Pakistan was shot in 1886. Except for the high Himalayas, the desert areas and Ceylon, the Indian tiger occupied the whole of India, Nepal, Sikkim, Bhutan, and western Burma, where it merged with the Indo-Chinese race along the north-south line of the Irrawaddy River. The total range today remains roughly the same, though the population has shrunk to a tiny fraction of its former size and is now fragmented into small groups scattered over an area nearly as large as Europe. Their isolation is so complete that an adequate interchange of genes is no longer possible. Where numbers are small, as they mostly are, degeneration is inevitable. To quote the Survival Service Commission of the IUCN: 'To maintain a genetic pool of sufficient variety in a population of animals such as the tiger, it is essential that a contiguous population of at least 300 should exist. All known populations in India are much smaller and the areas separating them are absolutely prohibitive to regular genetic exchange between them.

Hence in India no single population is now large enough to maintain a healthy stock.'

In 1930 it was estimated that there were still 40,000 tigers in the Indian subcontinent. In 1939 the figure was revised to 30,000. By the time of the Congress of the International Union for Conservation of Nature in New Delhi in 1969 it was announced by Shri K. S. Sankhala, at that time director of the Delhi Zoological Park, that the population had crashed to an unbelievable level of between 2,000 and 3,000. This was very close to the estimate of 2,800 made by Shri B. Seshadri in 1968, when he and I were trying to obtain international interest in the obviously appalling decline which was taking place. At least we had the satisfaction of seeing a resolution passed at the Congress, as a result of Sankhala's announcement, that the Indian tiger should be included in the IUCN *Red Book of Endangered Species*, where it joined the other races as meriting urgent international action.

Since then steps have been taken to verify these estimates by conducting more detailed population surveys. Such work takes time. In 1970 Richard Waller attempted a state-by-state assessment in collaboration with the Indian National Appeal of the World Wildlife Fund. He would be the last to pretend that this was a scientific survey, but by visiting all the reserves where tigers still occurred in India and by verifying the figures given by the game wardens in each state, he arrived at a total of 1,960. In 1972 the first detailed national survey was carried out for the Indian Board for Wildlife, by a skilled senior research officer, Shri S. R. Choudhury, and a team of carefully trained forestry officials. This was based on counting the pug-marks in every known tiger area. The imprint of the left hind foot of each tiger located was traced on a small glass screen and measured, to make sure that the same animal was not counted twice. The result, which can be taken as authoritative, showed that only 1,827 tigers remained in India.

Beyond the northern boundaries of India are the three small kingdoms of Nepal, Sikkim, and Bhutan, all of which were once rich in tigers of the Indian race. Today Nepal is thought to have a maximum of 150 and Bhutan perhaps a slightly larger number. Sikkim is a much smaller country, but it may still have a few tigers.

The area of what used to be East Pakistan, and is now Bangladesh, was once one of the best strongholds of the Indian tiger, particularly in the Sunderbans delta of the Ganges and Brahmaputra and in the Chittagong Hill Tracts. Perhaps one hundred survive in the Sunderbans. Elsewhere, the original forests which used to stretch from Mymensingh through Sylhet have nearly all disappeared; today the only tigers seen are occasional vagrants from Assam or Tripura. The Hill Tracts remained secure until the building of the Kaptai Dam, which was accompanied by the inevitable building of roads through the area. Huge tracts of primary forest were felled, or drowned by the new lake. Native settlements sprang up along the tributary rivers and shifting cultivation on the usual slash-and-burn technique followed. This process, in which crops are grown on the burnt ground which has been temporarily enriched by the nutrients in the fire ash, is the curse of all tropical regions. In spite of the luxuriant natural vegetation, tropical soil is notoriously impoverished and of poor value. Fire not only destroys the essential leaf litter but virtually sterilises the surface soil. The fertility of the ground is destroyed and within a couple of years must be abandoned. The horrible process is then repeated elsewhere and the whole environment is gradually debased and eroded.

Under these combined pressures the tigers of the Hill Tracts retreated across the Burmese frontier. Others were drowned by the flooding, or were shot. A few doubtless remain in the high forest behind Cox's Bazaar, but not many. The Mogh and Chakma tribesmen along the Karnaphuli River assured me that tigers still existed in the Pablakhali Reserve in 1966; but in many native languages the same name is given to the tiger and the leopard and we found evidence only of the latter.

4 Can the tiger be saved?

The problem of trying to save any animal which is nearing extinction is always fraught with great difficulties. In the case of the tiger these difficulties are formidable. The extensive losses of suitable habitat throughout its entire range can never be made good. The demand for land for agriculture and settlement will increase. Many of India's wildlife reserves already contain villages and thousands of domestic cattle, which deprive the tiger's wild prey of the grazing on which it depends. As the tiger loses living space and natural prey, so its predation on domestic livestock will inevitably increase. Where, as a consequence, tigers and leopards have been exterminated, heavy losses are now being suffered by farmers from uncontrollable numbers of wild deer and pigs, which are thus enabled to multiply unchecked. It is a vicious circle.

Hunting in the early days was done only by the rich, on foot or by elephant, and the tiger had a reasonable chance of surviving. With the advent of more accurate fire-arms and the go-anywhere jeep equipped with a spotlight for hunting at night, the balance swung against the tiger. By the time of World War II and Independence there was an extraordinary increase in the availability of guns throughout the subcontinent. Everyone could now have a go at the tiger. The common soldier or the villager could not only kill one, but in many instances could claim a bounty for doing so. Then came the internationally organised hunting tours, bringing eager sportsmen from the four corners of the earth to secure trophies. Prices for a guaranteed tiger rose to £1,000, and in 1970 one rich American is known to have paid £5,100 ($12,250) to secure his tiger.

Not surprisingly, the first steps to control hunting led to vigorous protests that those who organised the lucrative tiger *shikars* for visiting foreigners were being deprived of their livelihood. Asia has not yet reached the happy stage, which can be seen today in America and Britain, where hunting associations and conservationists co-operate to their mutual benefit. This is the more regrettable because many of Asia's hunters have extensive knowledge of wildlife which could be invaluable to the local conservation efforts. Nor should we forget that the stimulation of commercially organised tiger-hunting came largely from western countries.

As tigers became scarcer, the prices paid for their skins also soared. The big fashion houses were quick to jump on the bandwagon and began modelling tiger-skin coats with matching hats and handbags. These were vigorously promoted, first in the United States and later in Europe, as 'fun-furs' at prices of up to £1,000 a time. Overjoyed by the demand, the skin-traders of Asia gave financial backing to the poachers. When skins became scarce, the poachers moved into the Indian reserves and into neighbouring countries, making havoc particularly in Nepal. Today a poacher can get £50 for a good skin. The black-market dealer sells this for £200 or $500 to the tourist, who may be able to sell it back home, in certain countries, for double or treble this sum.

While this orgy of killing was in progress, a new threat to the tiger developed. Under the foreign aid programme, India and other countries were supplied with large quantities of toxic chemicals for agricultural use, such as Dieldrin, Endrin, DDT and the lethal defoliant Folidol. These were often given free to help peasant farmers. It did not take them, or the poachers, long to learn that such chemicals, sprinkled on the carcass of a cow, would ensure an agonising death for tigers, leopards, vultures and other animals which came to feed on it. A survey in the state of Madhya Pradesh alone showed that thirty-two tigers died from Folidol poisoning in eighteen months.

The new legislation against the export of skins is nevertheless beginning to take effect and there have been both confiscations at airports and prosecutions, which the World Wildlife Fund has publicised. But the task of controlling poaching and the black market in skins is an intractable one. Undeclared skins are easily concealed and there is no doubt that many are still being illegally smuggled by unscrupulous tourists, merchant seamen and airline staff.

Obviously the surest means of curing this evil is to kill the lucrative demand for skins. Some encouraging progress is being made. Discussion between the World

Wildlife Fund and the International Fur Trades Federation has led to an agreement that IFTF members in twenty-three countries would impose a voluntary ban on dealings in the skins of tigers, leopards, snow leopards and clouded leopards, all of which are listed in the IUCN *Red Book* as endangered. In support of this the Furriers Joint Council of the United States voluntarily agreed not to cut, fashion or fabricate any of these skins. It was a great step forward for conservation. Many leading fashion houses, sensitive to the change in public opinion, quickly co-operated by ceasing to display such skins and by promoting excellent man-made synthetics as an alternative.

There is now world-wide publicity about the parlous state of the endangered cats and also plenty of favourable comment about the new synthetic furs in magazines and the daily press. Everywhere women are beginning to recognise that it is no longer either chic or morally acceptable to wear skins of endangered animals. Young people are supporting the campaign and, indeed, on New York's Fifth Avenue have hissed women wearing real tiger-skin coats. Even the British armed services are helping, by agreeing to purchase no more tiger or leopard skins for their bandsmen's ceremonial aprons. Finally, governments of all the western nations have been asked by the World Wildlife Fund for a complete ban on the importation of these skins. Most of them have replied favourably and appropriate legislation is in preparation in some countries. But it will be a slow process. The United States have already imposed a ban on importations. Great Britain, through which more than 80 per cent of the world's furs pass, also forbids them, though regrettably still permitting the entry of made-up skin coats.

The need now in India and its neighbouring countries is to strangle the back-street black market, so that poachers cannot dispose of skins. Thousands of skins are held by small shopkeepers and black marketeers, and they are still openly offered for sale in all the hotels. Invariably they are said to have been obtained before the ban was introduced and at present the law is powerless to intervene. The obvious solution is for the State to buy up the stocks at wholesale prices and thereafter confiscate and prosecute if any skin is offered for sale. Skins of man-eaters or confirmed cattle-killers legally shot under licence should also automatically become State property. The wheels of government grind slowly and there are powerful commercial interests involved; but this critical loophole must be blocked if poaching is to be stopped. When big money is involved, every loophole will always be exploited by those who stand to gain.

Having examined the status of the various races of the tiger, a tentative 'survival table' might be drawn up as follows:

RACE	ESTIMATE OF NUMBERS SURVIVING
Indian tiger *P. t. tigris*	India 1,827; Bangladesh 100?; Nepal 150?; Bhutan 180?; Sikkim and west Burma a few. Could be saved by strenuous effort.
Siberian tiger *P. t. altaica*	Perhaps 130 left in Soviet Far East and a few in North-East China. Long-term survival doubtful.
Chinese tiger *P. t. amoyensis*	Scattered remnants being heavily persecuted. Extinction probable.
Indo-Chinese tiger *P. t. corbetti*	Perhaps 2,000 scattered over huge area, much of it devastated by war. Best chance of survival probably in Malaysia.
Caspian tiger *P. t. virgata*	Perhaps fifteen left in Iran only. Extinction probable.
Sumatran tiger *P. t. sumatrae*	In low hundreds and still persecuted. Long-term survival doubtful.
Javan tiger *P. t. sondaica*	Perhaps five to ten left. Extinction probable.
Bali tiger *P. t. balica*	Already extinct.

These estimates are my own and do not necessarily correspond with those published by official sources; but I believe them to be realistic. In the case of the apparently doomed Javan and Caspian races, it may still be possible

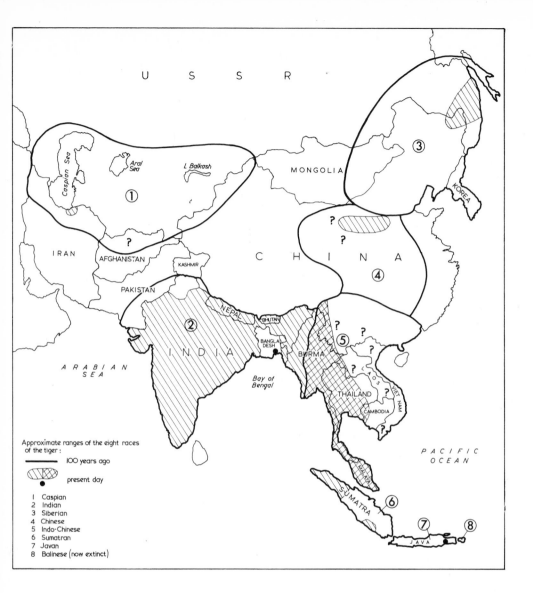

Approximate ranges of the eight races
of the tiger :

—————— 100 years ago

present day

1 Caspian
2 Indian
3 Siberian
4 Chinese
5 Indo-Chinese
6 Sumatran
7 Javan
8 Balinese (now extinct)

to save them if appropriate action can be taken in time.
As a last resort, it might even be possible to keep these
races intact by capturing the survivors and breeding
them in captivity, though this is an undesirable solution.
Several (though by no means all) of the leading zoos of
the world have established fine records of scientifically
controlled breeding of vanishing species and could be
relied upon to keep the stocks pure. In time they might
even be able to return the offspring to the wild if properly
managed reserves were by then available in the countries of origin. Several almost extinct species of other

33

animals have been saved by this means (Père David's Deer, Arabian Oryx, Néné Goose, etc) though not yet any of the great cats. It is not known, however, whether tigers reared in captivity would be capable of hunting their own prey – a process which in the wild requires two years' tutelage by their mothers.

5 Operation Tiger

During my time in Asia, studying the survival problems of the tiger, I had long discussions with Shrimati Indira Gandhi, Prime Minister of India, Sheikh Mujibur Rahman, Prime Minister of Bangladesh, and the late King Mahendra of Nepal. All three were intensely interested in saving the tiger, which they rightly regarded as part of the natural heritage of their respective countries. All three governments were already actively co-operating with the IUCN and WWF. Sheikh Mujibur had adopted the tiger as the symbol of Bangladesh and in India also it was the 'national animal'. Shrimati Gandhi had appealed in 1970 to all the Indian States to improve the protection of the species and all three countries had passed legislation banning tiger-hunting and the export of skins. At lectures and press conferences, I sensed a growing public indignation that tigers were nearing extinction. The press carried numerous articles and letters demanding that more effective action should be taken to save them. The time was obviously ripe for a major effort to be made. None of the many reserves where tigers still occurred was yet adequately equipped, nor managed to modern scientific standards. Concentration on those offering the best prospect of improvement and long-term security seemed the obvious solution. But close co-operation, great determination and speed of action would be essential if the tiger was to be saved.

At a joint meeting of the IUCN and WWF in Switzerland, I proposed an all-out international effort to create effective and fully equipped reserves in areas offering the optimum chances for the long-term survival of the tiger. These would have to be large enough to enable populations of at least one hundred tigers to be gradually built up in each reserve. As both time and available resources were inevitably limited, I proposed that all efforts should be concentrated on the one race of the tiger which still had sufficient numbers, and where there were fully co-operative local authorities; in other words, to help the governments of India, Bangladesh, Nepal and Bhutan to save the Indian race of the tiger. We could be confident that these governments would shoulder the major part of the work and of the financial burden involved, providing that the WWF could raise the money for all purchases involving foreign currency. These would include certain technical equipment and the salaries of specialists to help in training local people in wildlife management, ecological research and other essential techniques. Such a crash programme would require foreign currency amounting to about £400,000. I called the project 'Operation Tiger'.

In spite of many other world-wide demands for WWF funds for urgent conservation projects, my proposals were adopted. In October 1972 HRH Prince Bernhard of the Netherlands, President of the WWF, launched an appeal throughout the civilised world for funds for 'Operation Tiger'.

Shrimati Gandhi's reaction to our plans was characteristically swift and positive. She promised to form a special committee to co-ordinate action in India, which would report to her personally. To my astonishment, it was created the following morning, under the dynamic chairmanship of Dr Karan Singh, Minister for Tourism and chairman of the very active Indian Board for Wildlife. All of India's leading experts were on the committee, including the representative of the IUCN and WWF in India, Shri Zafar Futehally.

Working at top speed, the 'Tiger Task Force', as the committee came to be called, produced a bold and fully documented report in a remarkably short time. This called for nine special reserves (see Appendix), based on the improvement and enlargement of the best of the existing reserves. The budget, to be spread over the next five years, involved an investment by the Indian government equivalent to £2·1 million. Execution of this plan is already in operation. By its own initiative, India had launched the biggest wildlife conservation project ever seen in Asia.

Reaction to the WWF proposals in Bangladesh was similarly encouraging. President Choudhury and the Prime Minister promised that every effort would be made to improve the protection and development of the Sunderbans as a national park, in which Bangladesh's surviving tigers would be secure. WWF funds were urgently needed for patrol boats to control poaching and for trained ecologists to help in planning the management of the wildlife and vegetation.

The situation in Nepal was temporarily confused by the untimely death of King Mahendra, whose personal interest in the work of the WWF had been an inspiration to us. Nevertheless, when his son ascended the throne as King Birendra, we received assurances that Nepal's conservation efforts would continue unabated. In addition to the Chitawan and Sukla Phanta Tiger Reserves, there were hopes of a new one at Karnali, which is the best area for tigers in the country.

Bhutan, which still has a rather larger number of Indian tigers than Nepal, has also joined in the international effort and its fine Manas Reserve has been added to the list, thus bringing the total of reserves which will be improved to fourteen.

Saving the tiger is no longer a matter to be left to single nations – it is the responsibility of the whole civilised world. Like the man-made rock temples of Abu Simbel, which were saved at the last minute only by international effort and finance, the tiger, an irreplaceable natural treasure, *could* be saved. Not alone by the countries mentioned above, which are wrestling with the almost insurmountable task of providing for more than 700 million needy people, but by organised effort through the International Union for Conservation of Nature and its sister body the World Wildlife Fund. These are the two appropriate organisations to provide the technical and scientific know-how and to raise the foreign currency required. But the WWF, as a charitable foundation, is dependent on the general public for money. This money, though it has already achieved remarkable success in saving wildlife around the world, is always insufficient to keep pace with the flood of new projects which have been given top priority by the IUCN. Saving the tiger is only one of these. But it cannot wait. This is a project which needs and deserves support not only from the general public, but from other foundations and above all from governments. Otherwise it will be too late.

Many people who read this may share my view that preventing the loss of one of the world's best known and most beautiful animals is more important to our future generations than sending up yet another satellite to pollute outer space with our hardware. And it would cost infinitely less than this.

Will the effort be made? Or will the civilised world stand idly by and watch the tiger die? I believe we shall raise the necessary money and that we shall save at least the Indian race of the tiger. If we fail, our future generations will not lightly forgive us.

Portraits of the Indian tiger

The Indian tiger *Panthera tigris tigris*, though not the largest of the eight different races, is perhaps the most striking. Its colouration is a rich orange, with about eighteen to twenty black stripes from neck to tail root. The insides of the legs, the belly and around the face are white; the backs of the ears are black with a conspicuous white spot (the 'following signal' for cubs). Older males often have a pronounced ruff behind the cheeks, though much less prominently than in the Siberian race. The body is long, narrow and lithe. The muscular power is concentrated in the massive fore limbs, which are capable of pulling down a full-grown gaur weighing nearly a ton. The sight of an Indian tiger moving with infinite grace through the jungle is unforgettable. Not surprisingly this splendid animal has been chosen as a symbol of majesty by many kings and emperors.

Every tiger is different

When studying ti
in the wild, it is poss
to identify each
vidual animal by
characteristic pat
of black and w
marking above
eyes. Compare this
portrait with othe
the book to see
differences. There
also minor variat
in the striping or
body and legs.
ferences between
eight geograph
races of the tiger
in the coloura
striping, size, and
shape of the skull.
northern races
much longer and de
fur than those in
south.

The tiger's facial expressions

tiger's snarl is an expression of annoyance. A warning growl often precedes snarling – a deep mbling with the mouth closed. In snarling the mouth is opened and the lips partly drawn back to ose the teeth; the ears are partly flattened, the eyes narrowed and the tip of the tail is twitched m side to side. At high intensity of anger or fear the snarl may turn to hissing or an explosive tting, with the tail lashing, as in the domestic cat.

grimace occurs only when the tiger has been sniffing its own scent – the pungent liquid from anal glands which both sexes squirt on vegetation at frequent intervals to mark their tracks or itories. The whole face is wrinkled, the lips drawn back, the eyes half closed, the mouth opened the tongue invariably hung out. Lions have a very similar habit.

41

The tiger in the Sunder- bans

Tigers are very dependent on fresh water for drinking and bathing and they swim readily. In the Sunderbans mangrove jungle, in the deltas of the Ganges and Brahmaputra, they swim from island to island and have been known to cross as much as five miles of open water in the Bay of Bengal. Most of the Sunderbans water is highly saline and fresh water sources are scarce; part of the local tiger population has therefore adapted itself to drinking salt water. This is thought to have caused progressive physiological changes, including damage to the liver and kidneys, leading to unusually ferocious behaviour. It is known that since 1660 some, though certainly not all, Sunderbans tigers have been notorious man-killers, preying on honey-collectors, woodcutters and fishermen who penetrate the vast swamps. A study is now in process to discover whether, as seems likely, there is a correlation between the drinking of salt water and this persistent habit.

Power and majesty

Compared with the tiger, very few animals give such an immediate impression of majestic bearing and latent power. This portrait illustrates the tremendous mass of shoulder muscles and the great girth of the fore limbs. The tiger's retractable claws are just visible.

The tiger's camou- flage

In a cage, the tiger's colour scheme of orange, black and white looks very conspicuous, but in the animal's natural habitat, among patches of dark shadow and brilliant sunlight, it is a perfect combination. The transverse stripes on the tawny body break up its outline and provide an extremely effective camouflage. When standing in the high yellow grass which is typical of the forest glades where tigers seek their prey, or, as in the bottom picture, when lying in dappled sunlight among dead leaves, they are very difficult to distinguish. They use every shred of cover when stalking and their cryptic markings enable them to get close enough to make the final short rush on their prey successfully. Deer often smell a stalking tiger long before they see it; if the tiger remains hidden, they merely bark or stamp in alarm and then resume feeding, while the tiger moves cautiously closer.

Signs of the tiger

Being solitary and chiefly nocturnal, tigers are not easy to observe. However, their presence, even in dense jungle, can readily be detected by the signs they leave. Trees on which they sharpen their claws (*top*) are not difficult to see; the long scratches are usually higher and deeper than those of a leopard. Their pug-marks (*above*) on soft ground are also easily found. This is the footprint of an adult tigress. The size can be judged from the 6-inch spectacle-case beside it. Tracks of the sexes are distinguishable by the size of the 'palm', that of the male being larger and extending closer to the marks of the toes. The pug-mark of a leopard is often confused with that of a young tiger, but its toes are less widely separated from each other and from the 'palm' and are distinctly elongated. The tiger's imprint, even as a cub, is fractionally broader than long; the leopard's is the reverse.

45

The mating
of tigers

A pair of Indian tigers copulating in the New
Delhi Zoo, where captive animals enjoy unusually spacious enclosures. Tigresses in the
wild reach sexual maturity at about four years
of age, but in the abnormal conditions of captivity copulation has been observed as early
as two-and-a-half years. In temperate areas of
their range they come into breeding condition
seasonally, whereas in tropical regions they
are sexually receptive for about one week at
intervals of approximately one-and-a-half
months. The prelude to mating is accompanied
by periods of play and harmless sparring which
help to reduce the normal antagonism between the sexes. The copulatory act is very
brief, but is repeated many times for several
days. The tigress is seized by the scruff of the
neck, but rarely suffers the injuries which are
often inflicted by mating lions. The tiger
usually roars at the climax of mating.

Tiger cubs

The young are born blind, but their eyes open in fourteen days. They are weaned in about six weeks, although they remain largely dependent on their mothers for about two years. Cubs of the Indian race are usually born between November and April. Litters vary from one to six, or even seven, but seldom more than two or three survive from a large litter. If a litter is lost, the tigress is capable of producing a new one within five months; in captivity however, where the young are normally removed and hand-reared, a tigress has been known to have three litters within twelve months. In the wild it is doubtful whether even under favourable conditions the average tigress successfully raises more than one litter of two cubs to a state of independence every other year. Thus, although her reproductive potential is high, it can rarely be realised.

To the animal collector tiger cubs represent money, and they are eagerly sought. Nursing tigresses are frequently shot in order to obtain them and many cubs die in back-street bazaars or in transit to customers. The number of zoos and private collections of wild animals has more than doubled since the last World War and this has led to an additional threat to endangered species. However, the leading zoos of the world now have a very responsible attitude towards collecting and are helping conservation by agreeing not to seek any more animals listed by the International Union for Conservation of Nature in the *Red Book of Endangered Species*. But although there are plenty of tigers bred in captivity, commercial collectors still continue their lucrative trade, finding customers among the less responsible people who exhibit animals in order to make money, rather than to serve educational or scientific purposes.

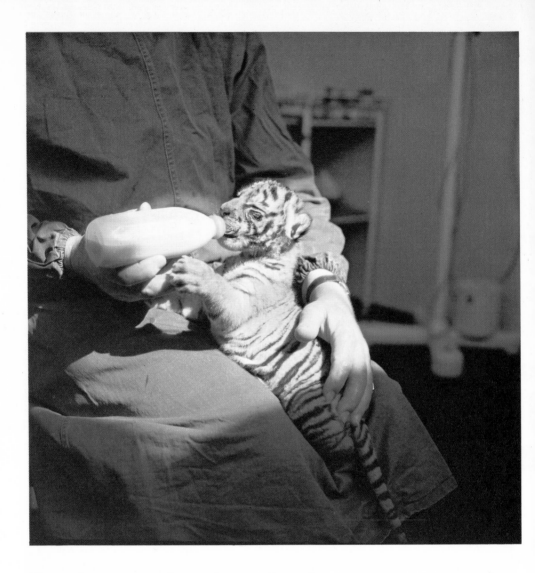

Rearing an abandoned cub

Hand-rearing an abandoned tiger cub at the London Zoo. Although tigers breed fairly readily in captivity, they have a lamentably bad record for abandoning or killing their young even when expertly managed and given minimum disturbance. Most cubs successfully born are therefore taken away from the tigress and have to be bottle-fed. Under the artificial conditions of captivity, matings are often unsuccessful because the tiger and tigress are usually together for only short periods. Disturbance and lack of privacy lead to a high incidence of pseudo-pregnancies, pre-natal and post-natal deaths, and the eating of cubs with the after-birth. Accurate statistics are not available concerning breeding success in the wild, but matings and births are probably often much more successful, though predation and accidents to the young take a heavy toll. Weaklings may survive with care in captivity, but never in the wild.

50

The importance of play

Like all the cats, young tigers spend a great deal of time playing. This is an essential element in the learning process. They are almost entirely dependent on their mothers for about two years and as soon as large enough accompany her on hunting forays, gradually learning how to catch their prey. Early efforts are clumsy and ineffective and the tigress has to do the killing. Even when nearly full grown, young tigers are often killed by wild boar or porcupines because of inexperience in hunting them. Weaklings soon die from inability to keep up with the family group; others fall victims to wild dogs, hyenas, jackals or crocodiles, are gored or trampled to death by cattle, or are killed by adult male tigers, which readily attack cubs of their own kind. Less than half of the wild cubs born reach full maturity.

Pulling down a buffalo

There have been many conflicting accounts of the way in which a tiger kills its prey. This remarkable photograph, taken by the American scientist George Schaller, shows a tigress and her nearly full-grown cub attacking a domestic buffalo. The tigress is pulling the buffalo down at the rump before seizing it by the throat to kill it. The cub, which has not yet been fully trained by the tigress, has gripped the buffalo's leg with its teeth; this would not necessarily bring down the animal or prevent it from goring the cub with its horns. Cubs take a long time to learn to kill efficiently and their early attempts are usually unsuccessful. Not until they have had repeated lessons from the tigress do they learn to go for the throat once the prey is pushed over.

A sambar deer is killed

An Indian tiger with a sambar which it has killed by seizing it by the throat, which is the usual method employed. Larger animals such as the gaur (the jungle bison) which can weigh five times the tiger's own weight, are first pulled down by the powerful fore paws and are killed either by a bite which breaks their necks or more often by being held by the throat until they strangle. By holding the gaur's head on the ground the tiger not only prevents it from regaining its feet and using its horns, but also avoids injury from being kicked during the death struggle. Tigers do most of their hunting between dusk and dawn, when the majority of their prey species also feed and are more likely to be caught in the open. Tigers may cover twenty miles a night in search of prey, following regular routes.

Behaviour in hot weather

During the height of the day tigers frequently leave their shady resting places to drink or cool themselves by standing submerged to the neck in a stream (*top*). The green grass, through which the Indian tiger in the lower picture is walking towards a stream, retains its colour for only a brief period in the tropics and for the remainder of the year is the same tawny shade as the tiger's coat. The picture shows the apparently very conspicuous white on the inside of the legs and on the belly. This has camouflage value, however, in helping to break up the shape of the tiger and merge it into its usual surroundings. A rounded shape in an overhead light is in shade on its lower surface and therefore retains a three-dimensional appearance; if it is coloured white below this minimises the shadow and flattens the image.

Do tigers chase their prey?

A captive Indian tiger leaping towards the photographer. In the wild such a sight would be terrifying, but this animal was not aggressive. Stories of tigers charging their prey in the open and seizing it with a spectacular leap are largely imaginary. They normally approach by stealth and when within a few paces rush on the victim from behind. Tigers are not fast runners and if the prey escapes the first rush it is rarely chased if it has any speed. Tigers are capable of jumping considerable heights and can scale high walls with apparent ease even when carrying heavy prey. They can also when necessary climb trees, and one hunter was seized by the leg when 18 feet up a tree. During the disastrous cyclone of 1969 in Bangladesh most of the tigers in the Sunderbans escaped the flooding by taking refuge in trees. Only six were found drowned.

Watching a herd of deer

Dawn and dusk are the best times for tiger-watching in the wild. If one remains hidden and silent, the tiger, like any other animal, can be observed going about its normal routine of hunting, feeding, bathing or resting. This picture of a tiger in evening light, shows it with raised head, watching a distant herd of deer coming out of the forest to feed in the meadow. Presently it will select the best route for approaching unseen and will then set off to stalk them through the long grass.

Indian tiger
in the snow

The Siberian tiger has been found in temperatures as low as −30°F, but it is not the only race which can live in the snow. The Indian tiger (*below*) and the Chinese tiger have also been recorded above the snow line. There is an authentic account of the tracks of an Indian tiger having been seen in deep snow in the Himalayas between Nepal and Sikkim at 13,000 feet above sea level.

A pair of tigers feeding

A tiger and tigress photographed at night while feeding on the carcass of a domestic buffalo. Unlike lions, which are highly social animals, tigers are solitary. Except when mating, they normally avoid each other. Occasionally, however, several adults will assemble when a large animal such as a buffalo or a gaur has been killed by one of them. All then defer to the dominant male and they treat each other with considerable caution, often sparring over the kill. On the other hand tigresses with cubs of up to two years old are frequently seen hunting or feeding together in obvious harmony.

The gaur

The gaur, or jungle bison, is one of the animals which tigers in India, Indo-China, Burma and Malaya prefer as their prey. The bull is a massive, humped animal, with short, curved horns and surprisingly small white feet, which look as if they are very inadequate to support a weight of as much as 2050 pounds. The gaur's usual habitat is hill forests, where there is ample coarse grazing in the valleys. By day the herds remain hidden in the trees, coming out at dusk to feed. The gaur is becoming increasingly scarce as Asia's forests diminish. The bull is a courageous animal, fully capable of intimidating a tiger if it can observe its approach in time. Nevertheless, many big bulls are killed by tigers, which stalk them from behind. Gaur herds will watch a tiger with curiosity rather than concern from a distance of 100 yards, but flee if it draws nearer.

The chital

Tigers find chital, or axis deer, a relatively easy prey where this species occurs. The buck carries big antlers, the record length being 39 inches. Often described as the most beautiful deer in the world, these handsome animals were once seen in large herds throughout most of the Indian subcontinent, from the foothills of the Himalayas to Ceylon. Today they survive in a wild state only in a few forested areas and wildlife reserves in India and Bangladesh. The destruction of forests, excessive hunting and the chital's susceptibility to rinderpest and tuberculosis have wiped them out elsewhere. The chital has a high, shrill bark. The white undersurface of the tail is prominently exposed in a series of high jumps to warn the herd if danger is near.

The barasingha

The barasingha, or marsh deer, is a handsome animal not unlike a red deer. Adult stags have antlers with ten or twelve tines. They have chestnut coats in summer, spotted with white along the spine and with white on the throat, rump and insides of the legs; the coat is blackish in winter. The barasingha was once a major source of food to the tiger. It occurred in the delta of the Indus in West Pakistan, in the Sunderbans of Bangladesh and along most of the Indian rivers. Today it survives only in small, scattered groups at the foot of the Himalayas in Uttar Pradesh, Nepal, North Bengal and Assam and in the central Indian state of Madhya Pradesh. The largest known population (about 1000) is in the Sukla Phanta reserve in Nepal. Poaching and reclamation of marshland for growing rice and sugar-cane have almost exterminated the species.

Sambar hinds

Sambar are also a frequent prey of the tiger. They have an extensive range in Asia, extending from China to Ceylon, the Malayan islands and the Philippines. They are the largest of the south-east Asian deer, record weights of stags exceeding 700 pounds. Adult stags bear large antlers with three tines; young ones have a single spike. The ears are large and the tail, which is much used vertically as an alarm signal, is rather long. The sambar's choice of forest habitat is very varied and it occurs not only in dry lowland woods but up to 12,000 feet in the Himalayan forests. Though chiefly nocturnal, a few sambar move about in the open during the rutting season. They have a loud barking alarm note and, like most other deer, also stamp the ground to warn the herd of danger. Herds, or family groups, are small, seldom exceeding six or eight individuals.

The jaws of the tiger

When a tiger yawns, one can appreciate its formidable array of teeth, which have been evolved for the purpose of tearing flesh, slicing through hide and crushing bones. The very long canines and powerful jaw muscles are essential for killing prey. The carnassial teeth (the fourth premolars above and the first molars below) are specially adapted to cutting skin, while the large molars are used for crunching. The meat is bolted rather than chewed and quite large bones are swallowed whole. The amount of food which a hungry tiger will consume at a single sitting may sometimes represent 60 pounds, or about one-fifth of its own weight.

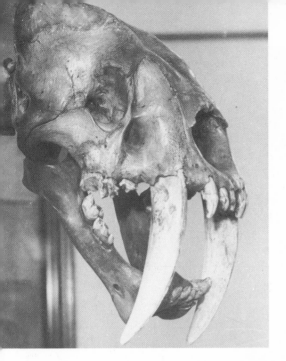

The sabre-toothed tiger

Nobody knows exactly what a sabre-toothed tiger looked like, though it is possible to obtain a general impression from fossil remains of the Lower Pliocene. It is, however, certain that it bore little resemblance to the tigers of today. It belonged to the now extinct genus *Machairodus*, which is generally regarded as a subfamily of the *Felidae*. The numerous species of this genus of carnivores occurred in the fauna of the late Tertiary in Europe, Asia, Africa and America. The sabre-toothed tiger was a large, powerful animal with enormous upper canine tusks (see *above*), which preyed on the thick-skinned, slow-moving herbivorous animals of the ice age: it became extinct just before the close of this. An exhibit in the Natural History Museum, London, on which this painting (*right*) by W. Backhouse is based, suggests an animal less heavily built than usually depicted. Today the nearest living relative of the sabre-tooth is probably the clouded leopard of Asia, which is a rather short-legged arboreal cat with long canines.

The tiger's sense of smell

Scent plays an important part in the daily life of a tiger, though, compared with sight, it is of only minor significance in hunting. As the tiger patrols its regular route through its hunting territory, it 'reads' with its nose the news of other tigers which have passed, by sniffing the scent which they leave at intervals on the vegetation. Fresh scent from a stranger can be the cause of alarm or caution; old scent means that the way ahead is unlikely to be challenged. The scent of a tigress in breeding condition is, of course, an immediate attraction to be followed by all males in the area.

66

Tigress in a poacher's trap

Throughout their entire range tigers are being shot, poisoned or trapped, either for the value of their skins, or because in the absence of their normal prey they are obliged to take village cattle. This Indian tigress was trapped by the toes in an illegally-set spring-trap. The ground is stripped bare of vegetation in the animal's desperate efforts to free itself. In spite of often heroic efforts by the guards, many tigers are poached inside reserves. The local wildlife authorities do their utmost to protect reserves, but have insufficient funds for the necessary number of wardens and vehicles, two-way radio sets, the construction of guard huts and patrol roads and other facilities which are required to overcome the highly organised and commercially-sponsored poaching.

Triumph for the hunter

The disappearance of Asia's once vast forests to make way for the rising human population was the primary cause of the tiger's catastrophic decline, but uncontrolled hunting was also a major factor. One Indian maharajah claimed to have shot 1,150 tigers and before Partition many hunters could claim to have killed more than 100. Commercially sponsored tiger hunts attracted sportsmen from every country and as the number of tigers declined new methods were introduced. Elephants and beaters were replaced by jeeps fitted with spotlights, which enabled hunters to shoot tigers much more easily at night. The slaughter thus intensified. Poaching, trapping and poisoning became rampant as the demand for tiger skins increased and the tiger was brought near to extinction. India, Bangladesh, Nepal, Bhutan and the USSR have now banned hunting and the export of skins, but losses continue in other countries where tigers still exist.

The
black
market
in skins

Scenes such as this are an all too familiar sight in the bazaars and hotel shops of south-east Asia. In spite of the ban on killing tigers or exporting their skins, and the ban on imports by Britain and America, poaching and the black market still thrive. Shopkeepers always say their stocks were acquired before the ban was introduced, but investigators posing as buyers report that dealers are still offering to supply as many as thirty fresh skins a month, well knowing that the tigers would be illegally killed. A solution would be for the governments to acquire all the skins in shops and thereafter prosecute anyone who offered them for sale. But commercial interests are involved and the cost would be great. Skins are mostly bought by foreign dealers or tourists rather than by local people. The ban on exports, if more rigidly applied, could prevent smuggling.

Siesta after hunting

An Indian tiger resting after a night's hunting. When satiated, tigers are lethargic and will doze in a secluded refuge throughout the heat of the day, interrupting their siestas only occasionally for a drink or a bathe in a nearby stream, plentiful fresh water being one of the essentials in their habitats. If hunting has been unsuccessful and prey is scarce, tigers may be forced by hunger to hunt in broad daylight, or to attack village cattle. At such times they will kill and eat a variety of insignificant creatures, including small birds and their eggs, snakes, lizards, frogs, fish and even termites. Examination of tiger droppings shows that they also often eat grass, bamboo leaves and berries. A good deal of soil is ingested while eating the carcasses of large animals. They prefer fresh meat, but will occasionally eat carrion.

The white tigers of Rewa

The white tigers of Rewa are unique. They are not true albinos (which have pink eyes), but are what scientists call 'recessive mutants'. They have brownish-grey stripes on a white background and bluish eyes. In 1951 a white male cub was trapped in the Rewa forest and kept by the local maharajah, who later mated it to a normal-coloured female, which produced three normal litters. A female from the second litter was then mated to the white tiger and in 1958 produced four white cubs with blue eyes. The delighted Maharajah of Rewa turned over his disused summer palace at Govindgarh to the tigers, which were carefully looked after. Later litters produced two white males and a normal female and then a white pair. The Indian government made an agreement to share the now famous white tigers as national treasures. Some of their offspring are prized exhibits in a number of Indian, European and American zoos. The original sire is now dead, but white tigers still live in the ancient palace. There is only one authentic record of a true albino tiger having been shot in India, but many reports during the past hundred years of pale or cream-coloured animals having been killed.

he man who
·ves tigers

an Aspinall has a remarkable rapport
h tigers and keeps no fewer than thirty-
of them on his estate near Canterbury.
record of success in breeding the
ian and Siberian races is probably un-
alled. By daily contact with them he has
ablished so intimate a relationship that
is able to take them for romps on the
ate (*left*), or for a swim with him in his
hing pool (*below*). They are not kept as
exhibits, nor taught to perform tricks,
are given optimum conditions to enjoy
. John Aspinall is an ardent conser-
ionist. As soon as fully secure wildlife
erves are available in Asia, he hopes
t offspring from his tiger collection can
introduced into them. The transition
m dependence on man to hunting their
n prey would be difficult, but perhaps
impossible to achieve under skilled
nagement.

Tigers as circus animals

Tigers bred in captivity can be trained to perform
acts such as jumping through hoops or rolling
over at a word of command. Nowadays little if any
cruelty is involved in training, though close con-
finement and often bad travelling conditions
leave much to be desired. The question of entertainment by performing animals is largely moral.
Children and perhaps the majority of adults
undoubtedly enjoy seeing tigers in circuses or
zoos, but there are those who question our right
to deprive animals such as the tiger of their
natural dignity, let alone their freedom. Tigers
in the wild are solitary, nocturnal and resent-
ful of the close approach of any other tiger
except when mating. The spectacle of a group
of circus tigers performing tricks before a noisy
crowd therefore cannot be claimed to have educational value. Tigers in cages become lethargic
and give little impression of their magnificence
in the wild.

73

An Indian tiger yawns while resting near a pool.

Tigers are dependent on water

Many zoos fail to realise how essential a bathing pool is to a tiger's enjoyment of life. The tiger pictured above was playing, executing a series of porpoise-like leaps half out of the water, to its obvious satisfaction. In very hot weather tigers often lie in shallow streams or pools, or go for a swim to cool themselves. During the long droughts which often occur in parts of Asia between the monsoon periods, they travel great distances in search of water and, if they cannot find it, dig holes for it in stream beds as shown in the picture below. Poachers are well aware of this need and either set traps at water-holes or poison them, even in protected reserves, in order to obtain tiger skins unblemished by bullet holes.

A tiger on patrol

Tigers regularly
roads or paths wh
have been construc
for the managemen
India's forests
often follow them
miles during
nightly patrol of t.
hunting ranges. See
their tracks, villa,
usually avoid using
paths at night. Th
are, however, many
counts of chance
counters with tiger
night and of villa,
making them turn
merely by shouting
them. But poacl
often lie in wait on
forestry roads and
the tigers easy tar,
when momenta
transfixed by a s
light. Jungle tra
regularly used by ti,
are chosen by na
hunters in many co
tries for the const
tion of pit-traps, w
are carefully car
flaged and lined v
split-bamboo spe
Another method i
suspend a heavy
armed with sp
above a clos
tethered pig, wit
trip-wire which
leases the log as
tiger takes the bait

The white hunter and his trophy

To shoot a tiger has been the ambition of most hunters. When tigers became scarce, sportsmen from all parts of the world hurried to obtain their trophies and hunting became big
business for the outfitters and hunting-tour operators. Hunting had little effect on the tiger
populations until the early part of the present century. After World War II the number of
fire-arms in Asia was multiplied a thousandfold and the pressure of hunting became excessive.
In spite of today's ban on hunting, the tiger populations are continuing to decline because of
poaching and the widespread use of poisoned bait. Thanks to the World Wildlife Fund, sixty
airlines have now agreed not to carry hunting parties which might endanger the survival of
rare species such as the tiger.

Tiger hunting as a sport

Hundreds of books about the joys of tiger hunting were published during the period of the British raj in India. These illustrations, taken from James Greenwood's *Wild Sports of the World* (1862) and William Rice's *Indian Game* (1884), are typical examples of the graphic manner in which the sport was treated. Tigers were plentiful in those days. The majority of the Indian princes and British army officers shot them as a favourite pastime and organised elaborate hunting parties for the entertainment of visitors. Towards the close of the epoch, however, many hunters were disquieted by the obvious decline in the tiger population. The famous Jim Corbett, renowned for his skill not only as a hunter but as a great naturalist, prophesied that the tiger would become extinct unless given protection. One of India's most beautiful national parks, in the Siwalik Hills, was later named after him.

£500,000 for a tiger painting

It is a curious reflection on human values that £500,000 was readily paid for Henri Rousseau's painting of a tiger, while strenuous efforts were having to be made throughout the civilised world to raise a similar sum to save the subject of the painting from becoming extinct. Collectors of rare paintings regarded the price paid for the National Gallery's acquisition as 'very reasonable', bearing in mind that one of Rousseau's paintings had already fetched $1 million in New York. There is seldom difficulty in raising money for such masterpieces or other man-made treasures, yet many irreplaceable natural treasures such as the tiger are allowed to disappear for lack of the necessary money to protect them. The World Wildlife Fund has declared that the tiger could be saved for posterity for the price paid for Rousseau's painting. It remains to be seen whether the public will regard the continued existence of the original animal as worth the cost of its very inaccurate nineteenth-century representation.

The Siberian tiger

The Siberian race of the tiger *Panthera tigris altaica* is a heavily built animal with dense fur enabling it to withstand the very low temperatures of northern Asia. Notable characteristics are the massive head with a fine ruffle around the cheeks and throat and the long hair on the belly in winter. The body colour is paler than in the southern races. Its chief food consists of moose, wapiti, roe deer, musk deer and sika deer, but it is also partial to bears, wolves, hazel hens and domestic animals including dogs. It is probable that the tiger species originated in the region of Siberia: as the range gradually extended southward the tigers became smaller, more richly coloured and with shorter fur appropriate to the high temperatures to which they had to adapt themselves. Adult male Siberian tigers weigh 650 pounds, whereas those in Sumatra or Java weigh as little as 350 pounds.

Death of an Indo-Chinese tiger

Shan hunters in Laos with an Indo-Chinese tiger *P. t. corbetti* which they have killed. This race of the tiger occupied an immense area stretching from southern China through Indo-China, Vietnam, Laos, Cambodia, eastern Burma, Thailand and Malaysia to the outskirts of Singapore. Once very numerous, it has suffered heavy losses throughout its range in recent years. Many vast forested areas in most of these countries have been devastated by modern warfare, not only by artillery and massive bombing with high explosives from the air, but also by napalm and by saturation with arsenical defoliants, from which neither wildlife nor humans could survive. Only in Malaysia is the Indo-Chinese tiger still holding its own, with a population last estimated at 600. But even in that country forests are disappearing under commercial exploitation and the tiger's living space, particularly in the lowlands, is threatened.

How to gain the tiger's courage

Tiger-meat for a hunter and his family. In many parts of south-east Asia the belief persists that by eating the raw flesh of a tiger the hunter will gain the animal's strength and courage. In China, not only the flesh but the blood and ground-up bones of the tiger are relished by primitive peasants in the belief that they confer either courage or hold aphrodisiac qualities. This custom, and the official statement by the Chinese government that the tiger is 'a hindrance to agricultural and pastoral progress', are sufficient to ensure that the Chinese tiger *P. t. amoyensis* will not survive for long. Nobody knows how many remain, apart from a Chinese report that they are now 'very rare'.

The Sumatran tiger

The Sumatran tiger *P. t. sumatrae*, here photographed in the Prague zoo, is smaller and more fully striped than the northern races and its skull has a distinctively flattened profile. Until 1936 it was a common animal even near the densely populated areas of Sumatra, but twenty years later its numbers were steeply declining. Today it survives only in the northern part of the island and in the mountainous regions of the south-west. The destruction of its formerly secluded forest habitat and of its natural prey species has obliged the Sumatran tiger to prey increasingly on village livestock. In consequence it is constantly hunted and trapped in baited pitfalls armed with bamboo spears. Unless it is given effective protection, the survival of this race is very doubtful.

A photograph of the skin of a Bali tiger *P. t. balica*. It was believed that the last known specimen seen in the wild was shot in 1937, but in 1972 there was an unconfirmed report that another one had been sighted. In 1914 the Bali tiger was reported to be still common on the island, but by 1920 it had become rare. No attempt was made to save the remaining population. This unique race, representing the southern-most extension of the range of the species, was declared by the Indonesian authorities to be extinct in 1973.

The last of the Javan tigers?

According to latest information there are probably only five to ten Javan tigers *P. t. sondaica* surviving in the wild. This recent amateur photograph may therefore have historic value. It shows the characteristic narrow striping of the Javan race. The shape of the skull differs slightly from those of the other races. The Javan tiger was common throughout the island in 1851. The native population regarded it as the reincarnation of the souls of their ancestors. One would therefore expect the tiger to be held in reverence and to be strictly protected. On the contrary it has been enthusiastically hunted and by the 1930s had become rare. By 1955 only about twenty-five were left. Today the few survivors are protected in the Betiri forest reserve, but their chances of perpetuating this unique race are slender.

The tiger's toilet

Like all the cats, a healthy tiger spends a good deal of time grooming itself. After killing and eating its prey, its face and fore limbs are usually covered with gore which is scrupulously licked off before the tiger goes to rest, otherwise it would be tormented by flies. If it cannot finish a carcass at a single sitting, it often covers it with earth and grass to prevent it from being found by vultures and jackals, though this precaution is usually unsuccessful. Tigers also have a habit of scraping earth with their hind feet to hide their droppings, but, as this is purely ritualised behaviour, the droppings are seldom covered.

Hunting in a reed bed

During the daylight hours tigers are usually inactive, resting in the
shade. In very hot weather they often lie in swampy reed beds near
water, where they can slake their thirst or go for a dip at intervals.
It is very obvious that they do not enjoy extreme heat. They are not
averse to mud and their tracks are often seen in the very soft mud of
mangrove swamps, where they catch fish, frogs and crabs in the
shallow water. In spite of their size and weight, tigers can move
through reed beds with extraordinary skill in avoiding detection
when stalking, and are thus able to catch animals such as hog deer
and wild boar which frequently shelter in them.

Can the tiger be saved?

Of all the world's wild animals, the tiger is one of the best known and one of the most magnificent. Yet it has now been persecuted to the verge of extinction throughout its entire range. It is one of the most important animals in Asia in restricting the populations of deer and wild boar, which, without its influence, would multiply to such an extent as to endanger agriculture – as is already apparent in areas where the tiger has been exterminated. If the tiger follows the dodo into oblivion, the world will have lost one of its greatest natural treasures. A strenuous international effort is now being made by the World Wildlife Fund to help the governments of countries where tigers still occur, to create fourteen scientifically managed reserves where, under complete protection, they·may yet survive for the enjoyment of posterity.

Appendix: Summary of information about the tiger

1 THE SPECIES

The tiger species *Panthera tigris* is divided into subspecies, or races, each differing in minor degree, such as colouration, striping, shape of skull, or length of fur. The following are usually recognised, though some authors merge several races, or further subdivide them: Indian *P. t. tigris*; Siberian *P. t. altaica*; Chinese *P. t. amoyensis*; Indo-Chinese *P. t. corbetti*; Caspian *P. t. virgata*; Sumatran *P. t. sumatrae*; Javan *P. t. sondaica*; Balinese *P. t. balica*.

2 DIMENSIONS AND WEIGHTS

Males are larger and heavier than females in all races. The largest is the Siberian, which is reported to have reached a record length of 13 ft and a weight of 750 lb. These figures are not authenticated however. Schaller (1967), quoting reliable records, gives the maximum length of a tiger shot in the wild as 10 ft 3 in and the greatest reliably recorded weight as 705 lb. The average for the Indian race is about 9 ft 6 in and 450 lb for a full grown male, and 8 ft and 300 lb for a female, though there is considerable variation. Tigers of the southern races are smaller and more closely marked.

3 HABITAT

Tigers are very adaptable. In different parts of their range they occupy a wide variety of habitats. Their chief requirements are ample cover for stalking, a sufficiency of prey, and water for drinking and bathing. In different countries they are found in high coniferous and lowland deciduous forest, scrub and reed thickets, mangrove swamps, dry thorn forest and rain forest. In Manchuria they withstand temperatures as low as −30°F and their tracks have been found in snow at 13,000 ft in the Himalayas.

4 RANGE AND PRESENT DISTRIBUTION

Nobody knows exactly the original range of the various races, nor can the present ranges of the mainland races be plotted accurately, owing to lack of reliable information. The map on p. 33 is approximate. It indicates only where some tigers of the races indicated are thought still to survive.

5 PRESENT POPULATIONS

There were probably still at least 100,000 tigers of the various races in Asia at the time of World War I. Today the total of all races does not exceed 5,000, broken down as follows:

Indian race

In India 1,827; Bangladesh about 100; Nepal about 150; Bhutan about 180; Sikkim and west Burma a few. Total about 2,300.

Siberian race

About 130 in Soviet Far East; possibly a few in north-east China.

Chinese race

Reported only as 'very rare' and rapidly being exterminated as official policy.

Indo-Chinese race

No reliable information from most of its range. Probably exterminated in the various war zones. Scattered over a huge area perhaps 2,000 remain, of which 600 are in Malaysia.

Caspian race

Perhaps fifteen, in Iran only.

Sumatran race

No reliable information. Believed to be in low hundreds.

Javan race

Perhaps five to ten left.

Balinese race

Now extinct.

6   REASONS FOR DECLINE

Entirely caused by human influences. Chiefly the destruction of the tiger's forest habitat and prey species; secondly, excessive hunting, trapping or poisoning, for sport, the sale of skins, or for the protection of domestic livestock.

7   REPRODUCTION AND LONGEVITY

Information concerning tigers in the wild is scanty, though zoo records are plentiful. Wild tigresses reach sexual maturity in two to four years, but in captivity have bred in two years. Breeding is promiscuous and males take no part in rearing the cubs. There is no fixed mating or cubbing season. The gestation period varies from 95 to 109 days. Litters vary from one to an exceptional seven, but it is unusual in the wild for more than two or three cubs to survive. Schaller (1967) has shown that if a wild tigress loses her litter, it is possible for her to produce another in about five months. On average cubs are reared successfully to maturity only once in two-and-a-half years (a replacement rate of six to seven adults in the tigress's lifetime). Cubs stay with the tigress for about two years, being taught how to hunt. Tigers have lived for twenty years in zoos, but in the wild under today's conditions are very unlikely to survive that long.

8   FEEDING HABITS

Tigers are solitary and largely nocturnal animals. They kill about twice a week, or more often if only small prey is available. They kill anything they can catch – mammals (including other carnivores), birds, reptiles, or fish; occasionally they eat vegetation, but rarely carrion. Preferred prey is hoofed animals such as deer, wild oxen and wild boar. Domestic cattle are frequently taken. Prey is stalked and, when close enough, seized by the throat or the nape of the neck, large animals being toppled over with the powerful fore paws. Carcasses of up to 500 lb are easily dragged for several hundred feet before being eaten. More than 60 lb of meat can be consumed at a single sitting. Hunting ranges are patrolled at night for distances of up to twenty miles.

9   MAN-EATING

Tigers try to avoid contact with man and are not inherently aggressive towards him. Man-eating is an exceptional habit, usually occurring only when tigers are no longer able to hunt their natural prey because of infirmity or injury. The only area where man-eating has become an established habit is in parts of the saline swamps of the Sunderbans, where it is thought that physiological changes have been caused by the constant ingestion of salt water. Twenty times more people in India die of snake-bites than from man-eating tigers.

10 NUMBERS OF TIGERS SHOT

Records kept by hunters suggest that the number of tigers shot for sport between 1850 and 1950 must have run into tens of thousands. Single individuals, chiefly British, Indian or Nepalese, not infrequently killed totals exceeding 300. The Maharaja of Udaipur shot at least 1,000; the Maharaja of Surguja claimed to have shot 1,150 by 1965. In 1911 King George V and his party shot thirty-nine tigers in eleven days in Nepal. Although hunting is now banned, tigers are still being shot, poisoned, or trapped by poachers. In China they are being deliberately exterminated.

11 PROTECTIVE MEASURES TAKEN

Most of the countries where tigers still survive now prohibit tiger hunting and the export of skins. The United States and Britain have banned imports. Other western countries are expected to follow suit. Most fashionable women now regard wearing the skins of endangered animals as no longer socially acceptable. The International Fur Trades Federation has asked its members in twenty-three countries to accept a voluntary ban on the sale of skins of tigers and other endangered animals. The Furriers Joint Council of the United States has agreed not to make up any of these skins. Sixty airlines have now signed a pledge prepared by the WWF, undertaking not to promote or carry hunting tours involving the killing of endangered species such as the tiger. Special reserves for the tiger are now being created in Asia (see below).

12 SPECIAL TIGER RESERVES

Many countries where tigers occur have reserves which give some protection. Many of these are, however, poorly managed, inadequately protected, or too small. The WWF has now organised a world-wide campaign to raise funds to help the governments of India, Bangladesh, Nepal and Bhutan to save the Indian tiger from extinction by the creation of fourteen large, scientifically managed reserves, in each of which it is hoped to build up populations to at least one hundred tigers. The following list shows in brackets the present numbers of tigers in these reserves, where known:

India	The Manas Reserve, in Assam (40)
	The Palamau National Park, in Bihar (37)
	The Simlipal Reserve, in Orissa (?)
	The Corbett National Park, in Uttar Pradesh (30)
	The Ranthambore Reserve, in Rajasthan (14)
	The Kanha National Park, in Madhya Pradesh (36)
	The Melghat Reserve, in Maharashtra (?)
	The Bandipur Reserve, in Mysore (18)
	The Sunderbans Reserve, in West Bengal (27)
Bangladesh	The Sunderbans Reserve (100)
Nepal	The Chitawan Reserve (12)
	The Sukla Phanta Reserve (15)
	The Karnali Reserve (?)
Bhutan	The Bhutan Manas Reserve (?)

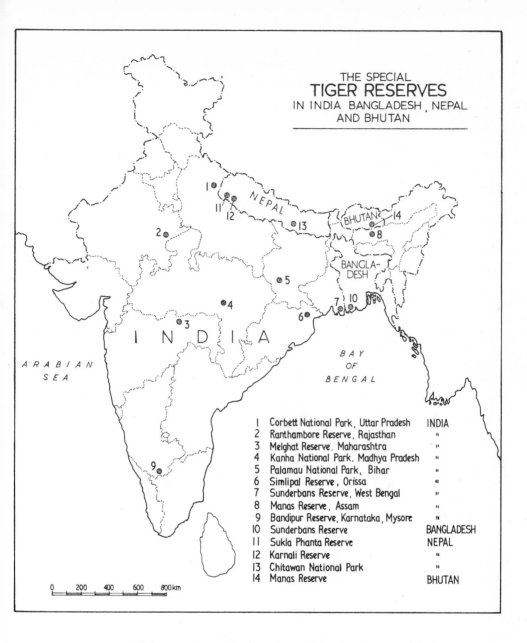

THE SPECIAL
TIGER RESERVES
IN INDIA BANGLADESH, NEPAL
AND BHUTAN

1	Corbett National Park, Uttar Pradesh	INDIA
2	Ranthambore Reserve, Rajasthan	"
3	Melghat Reserve, Maharashtra	"
4	Kanha National Park, Madhya Pradesh	"
5	Palamau National Park, Bihar	"
6	Simlipal Reserve, Orissa	"
7	Sunderbans Reserve, West Bengal	"
8	Manas Reserve, Assam	"
9	Bandipur Reserve, Karnataka, Mysore	"
10	Sunderbans Reserve	BANGLADESH
11	Sukla Phanta Reserve	NEPAL
12	Karnali Reserve	"
13	Chitawan National Park	"
14	Manas Reserve	BHUTAN

This map shows the locations of the fourteen special tiger reserves
which the governments of India, Bangladesh, Nepal and Bhutan are
now creating or improving. By far the largest part of the cost involved
will be borne by these governments. The World Wildlife Fund has
undertaken to raise £400,000 for the purchase of technical and
scientific equipment which will be needed to control poaching and for
the effective management of the reserves.

93

Selected bibliography

ALLEN, H. *The Lonely Tiger* (1960).

ANON. 'Mammals in Danger of Extinction', *Oryx*, vol 7, no 5 (1964), 226–8.

ANON. 'Poison for Indian Tigers and Leopards', *Oryx*, vol 8, no 2 (1965), 75.

BAIKOV, N. *The Manchurian Tiger* (1925).

BAZE, W. *Tiger! Tiger!* (1957).

BERG, B. *Tiger und Mensch* (Berlin, 1936).

BURTON, M. *Systematic Dictionary of Mammals of the World* (1962).

BURTON, R. *The Book of the Tiger* (Boston, 1933).

BURTON, R. *The Tiger Hunters* (1936).

CHAMPION, F. *With a Camera in Tiger-land* (1927).

CORBETT, J. *Maneaters of Kumaon* (1944).

CORBETT, J. *Man-eaters of India* (1957).

CROWE, P. K. *The Empty Ark* (New York, 1967).

DANG, H. 'The Future of the Tiger', *Cheetal*, vol 5, no 1 (1962), 46–7.

DENIS, A. *Cats of the World* (1964).

FISHER, J., SIMON, N., and VINCENT, J. *The Red Book – Wildlife in Danger* (1969).

FITTER, R., and LEIGH-PEMBERTON, J. *Vanishing Wild Animals of the World* (1968).

FLETCHER, F. *Sport on the Nilgiris and in Wynaad* (1911).

FORSYTH, J. *The Highlands of Central India* (1889).

GEE, E. P. *The Wildlife of India* (1964).

INDIAN BOARD FOR WILDLIFE (Government of India). *Project Tiger* (New Delhi, 1972).

LYDEKKER, R. *The Game Animals of India, Burma, Malaya and Tibet* (1924).

MORRIS, D. *The Mammals* (1965).

MOUNTFORT, G. *The Vanishing Jungle* (1969).

MOUNTFORT, G. 'The Bengal Tiger Enters the Red Book', *Animals*, vol 13, no 3 (1970), 110–12.

NOVIKOV, G. *Carnivorous Mammals of the Fauna of the USSR* (Washington DC, 1962).

O'BRIEN, E. 'Where man-eating tigers occur', *J Bombay Nat Hist Soc*, vol 45, no 1 (1944), 231–2.

PERRY, R. *The World of the Tiger* (1964).

POCOCK, R. 'Tigers', *J Bombay Nat Hist Soc*, vol 33, no 3 (1929), 505–41.

POCOCK, R. *The Fauna of British India: Mammalia* (1939).

POWELL, A. *Call of the Tiger* (1957).

PRATER, S. *The Book of Indian Animals* (Bombay Nat Hist Soc: Bombay, 1948).

SCHALLER, G. 'My Year with the Tigers', *Life*, vol 58, no 25 (1965), 60–6.

SCHALLER, G. *The Deer and the Tiger* (Chicago, 1967).

SESHADRI, B. 'New Hope for the Tiger', *Country Life*, vol CLIV (1973), 1714–6.

SIMON, N., *et al. Red Data Book (1) Mammalia* (IUCN: Lausanne, 1966).

SIMON, N., and GÉROUDET, P. *Last Survivors* (1970).

SINGH, K. *The Tiger of Rajasthan* (1959).

SOMERVILLE, A. *The Home of the Man-eater* (Calcutta, 1933).

STERNDALE, R. *Natural History of Indian Mammals* (1884).

STEWART, A. *Tigers and Other Game* (1928).

STRACEY, P. 'The Future of the Tiger', *Cheetal*, vol 3, no 2 (1961), 29–32.

TALBOT, L. *A look at threatened species* (Fauna Preservation Society: London, 1960).

WALLER, R. 'Last chance for the tiger?', *Animals*, vol 13, no 16 (1971), 748–51.

Acknowledgements

William Backhouse (artist) 65b
Tony Beamish 83
British Museum (Natural History) 65t
L. R. Condoux 82
Conway Maritime Press 70, 77
E. P. Gee 39t, 63t, 88–9
Wallace Heaton 72t and b
Indonesian Institute of Biology 85t and b
Peter Jackson, Bruce Coleman Ltd 46–7, 55t, 62t, 63b, 71t
Keystone Press Agency 42t, 48
M. Krishnan 68
Frank W. Lane 40, 64
London Library 78t and b
Hugh Maynard 60–1, 87
Guy Mountfort 62b
National Gallery 79
Odhams Press 73
Okapia 49, 54, 84
Omslap 76
James Osbourne 80, 81t
George Schaller 44t
George Schaller, Bruce Coleman Inc 52–3, 58
Adolf Schmidecker 43, 51, 66, 81b
W. Schrame, Jacana 59
Richard Walter, AFA Colour Library 39b, 41t and b, 42b, 45t and b, 55b, 56–7, 71b, 75t and b, 86b
Zoological Society of London 50
Christian Zuber, WWF 67, 69
Nadine Zuber 74

Index